AN AUTISM DIAGNOSIS MUST COME FROM A LICENSED PROFESSIONAL

OUR MISSION:

SHARE THAT EVERY CHILD ON THE AUTISM SPECTRUM IS UNIQUE, BUT NOT ALONE.

PROVIDE A CREATIVE OUTLET FOR AUTISTIC CHILDREN TO LEARN ABOUT THEMSELVES.

SPREAD AUTISM AWARENESS THROUGH RELATABLE REAL LIFE SCENARIOS TO FOSTER STRONGER RELATIONSHIPS IN THEIR COMMUNITY.

"Nacho is on the Spectrum" Text and Illustrations © 2024
ALL RIGHTS RESERVED BY JEI PRODUCTIONS LLC
FIRST EDITION, 2024

This book is not intended as a substitute for medical advice. The reader should consult a licensed professional in matters relating to their health, particularly with respect to any symptoms that may require diagnosis or medical attention.
No part of this book may be used or reproduced in any manner whatsoever without written permission except in the case of brief quotations embodied in clerical articles and reviews.
All characters appearing in this work are fictitious. Any resemblance to real persons, living or dead, is purely coincidental.

Publisher's Cataloging-in-Publication
(Provided by Cassidy Cataloguing Services, Inc.)

Names: Martinez, Jason, author. | Martinez, Isaac, 2014- author. | Paj, Eduardo, illustrator.

Title: Nacho is on the spectrum / written by Jason Martinez and Isaac Martinez ; illustrated by Eduardo Paj.

Description: First edition. | [Arvada, Colorado] : JEI Productions LLC, [2024] | Series: Kids spectrum stories. | Audience: Elementary school children. | Summary: With some help from his dad, Nacho writes about being on the Autism Spectrum and what it has meant for him. In his story, Nacho opens up about the things that are hard, what it was like to be diagnosed, and how he found comfort in learning more about himself.—Publisher.

Identifiers: ISBN: 979-8-9899915-0-1 (Paperback) | 979-8-9899915-1-8 (Hardcover) | LCCN: 2024905848

Subjects: LCSH: Autism in children--Juvenile literature. | Autism in children--Treatment--Juvenile literature. | Autism spectrum disorders in children--Juvenile literature. | Senses and sensation--Juvenile literature. | CYAC: Autism. | Senses and sensation. | LCGFT: Picture books. | BISAC: FAMILY & RELATIONSHIPS / Autism Spectrum Disorders. | FAMILY & RELATIONSHIPS / Children with Special Needs. | PSYCHOLOGY / Psy-chopathology / Autism Spectrum Disorders.

Classification: LCC RJ506.A9 M37 2024 | DDC: 616.85/882--dc23

Learn more about us at www.kidsspectrumstories.com

NACHO
is on the Spectrum

Written by Jason Martinez and Isaac Martinez
Illustrated by Eduardo Paj

Hi, I'm Nacho.

Talking can be hard for me,

but I love to read and write.

My dad helped me write a story about myself.

Can I read it to you?

Yay!

Since I was a puppy, I could tell that my mind and body worked differently.

How, you ask?

Well...

The world is too bright and too loud.

It's really hard for me when things change.

Sometimes my fur feels really itchy

and I don't like getting wet.

I have to try really hard to keep my body calm.

If I can't stay calm, sometimes I yell, cry, freeze, wiggle my body, or forget how to use my words.

There are times when others get upset with me,

and that makes me sad.

I am doing my best.

One day after school, my parents took me to a special doctor.

She asked our family a lot of questions.

(So many questions!)

After she was done, we learned that

I am on the Autism Spectrum.

I didn't know what that meant.

But it helped my family and friends

learn more about me.

Everyone showed how much they cared

and wanted to help.

To be honest, I didn't like the extra attention.

But it was worth it.

We started doing things that really helped me.

A few of my favorites are taking breaks in quiet places and having an easy-to-read schedule.

I'm learning new things about my autism everyday.

www.ingramcontent.com/pod-product-compliance
Lightning Source LLC
Chambersburg PA
CBHW060654060526
44119CB00076B/234